Dedicated to Adrian, Camila, Levy & Vida
who always show me that a rainy day is a fun
day.

Camila & the Rain

by Clara Torres-Jamison

Illustrated by Chad Vivas

Camila looked outside and saw little drops of rain falling on her window.

"Awww," she said.

"how I wish this rain would go away."

The rain fell harder and harder.

She went to the kitchen, and remembered the yummy, goeey chocolate chips cookies she made with her Mami earlier that day.

"Oh, yum!" she said excited.

But when she opened the jar...

"Aw man! Who ate my cookies?" Camila asked confused.
"I bet Lucas ate them!"

She tip-toed to Lucas' room and peeked inside.

He was playing his drum.

"Oooh, can I play?" she asked curiously.

"Sure!" he said.

She tried playing with the drum and well... it didn't go as planned.
"HAH! MY DRUM!" Lucas shrieked.

SORRY...

Camila felt so bad that she gave him a
big "sorry" hug.

"I'll fix it," he said with a faint smile, "it's ok."

Camila walked to the living room, and saw her mother
sitting on the big fluffy couch.

Mami! Can
you play with
me?

"I was thinking we can paint,"
Camila said optimistically.

"Ok," Camila said sadly.

"Perhaps, dad will play with you on the computer,"
her Mami suggested as Camila walked away.

Camila skipped into her father's itty bitty office

Dad?! Can we play on the computer?

"Mmmhmmm!" he said, but never lifted his eyes away from the screen or even moved.

"Oh, brother!" she thought.

"Maybe Luna would like to come over and play?"

Luna was Camila's best friend in the whole wide world.

But when she called Luna to come over to play:

"Sorry, Cami, but I am creating a video, can we play later?"

"Okay," Camila replied with a frown.

Camila went back to her room to play with Teddy.

But Teddy was NOT in the mood.

No matter what she tried to do, nothing was working and the rain kept falling.

"Hmmm...," she thought, "how I wish this rain would stop and go away."

Rain, rain go away!

But then...

She got an IDEA!

"Where are my rain boots?!" Camila shouted as she looked for her rain coat.

"In the closet. Why do you need it?" Mami replied.

"Because, I am going to *shoo* the rain to go away."
Camila said excited.

Outside, as the rain fell, Camila wiggled her body from side to side, moved her hands like waves and began singing:

"Rain, rain go away! Come again another day!"

The rain fell harder
AND HARDER.

Just then she got a BETTER IDEA...

She slid down the mud,

made MUD PIES,

and made RAIN MUSIC
with her POTS and
PANS.

Camila was having so much fun that everyone took notice and one by one...

they joined her...

caught rain drops on their tongues,

It was so much FUN
that they forgot all about the rain!

And when the sun peaked out of the clouds,

Camila quickly sang... as she wiggled her body from side to side and moved her hands like waves:

"Rain, rain
come again,
come and play
back again!"

Clara

TORRES- JAMISON

AUTHOR

Clara Torres-Jamison is a multi-media storyteller, speaker, sales and marketing veteran, serial entrepreneur, and mom of 4. She is a lover of questions and believes that everyone's power begins with the hardest action of accepting oneself & others as they are (not what we want them to be).

Storytelling has always been her passion and her escape.

She loves the outdoors and everything behavioral science. She has been certified in wellness, social and emotional learning, ADHD coaching, Adult, Kids & Trauma Yoga and much more.

She founded Resiliency Group LLC, as a social change agency to help individuals understand that their past doesn't define them and to create stories that are catalyst of change and action.

JOIN HER IN TEACHING KIDS & ADULTS ABOUT FLEXIBLE THINKING, RESILIENCY, MOVEMENT, S.E.L & MORE!

@CLARAMAZING
E: CLARA@RESILIENCYGROUPLLC.COM
WWW.CLARAJAMISON.COM

Made in the USA
Middletown, DE
21 August 2020